Chapter 1

Introduction

False Sense of Security

James W. Archer, D.C.J.

Archway Publishing books may be ordered
through booksellers or by contacting:

Archway Publishing
1663 Liberty Drive
Bloomington, IN 47403
www.archwaypublishing.com
844-669-3957

ISBN: 978-1-6657-1869-1 (sc)
ISBN: 978-1-6657-1870-7 (hc)
ISBN: 978-1-6657-1868-4 (e)

Library of Congress Control Number: 2022902261

Print information available on the last page.

Archway Publishing rev. date: 2/21/2022

Contents

Background

Sex offender residency restrictions have been widely used since the 1990s throughout the United States with the intention of preventing repeat sexual assaults from convicted sex offenders, especially child sexual assault victims, by enforcing geographic boundaries where sex offenders can live, and places where they can visit, usually in the hundreds of feet up to thousands of feet (Budd, 2016). The problem with sex offender residency restrictions, are that they do not protect most child victims of sexual assault from occurring and as of this time there is no evidence that has been produced to show they produce a reduction in sex offender recidivism (Budd, 2016).

A considerable amount of research exists showing that the vast majority of sexual assaults happen inside the home of the child or inside the home of a close family friend or relative. These people are often not suspected of being a potential predator, so quite often they are given unfettered access to small, innocent, and trusting children (Bratina, 2013).

The violent and disturbing nature of sex offenses and political and public pressure motivate state and local entities to put in place restrictive policies and laws that are designed to restrict and prohibit certain sex offenders from being within so many feet of schools, parks, playgrounds, daycare centers, and other areas where children may congregate. The physical distance of these restrictions varies from state to state, but typically sex offenders are prohibited from living, working, and visiting within five hundred to two thousand feet of designated areas. (Bratina, 2013).

According to Bratina (2013), the problem with sex offender residency restrictions is that they restrict or prohibit an individual with a previous sexual criminal history of offenses against children from being within a specified distance (usually between five hundred to two thousand feet) of a school, park, playground, daycare center, or other areas where children may congregate, with the hope that the child sexual predator will not have an opportunity to select a victim in one of these areas. Although there are cases where children are abducted from one of these public areas and sexually assaulted and sometimes murdered by a stranger, the research shows that approximately 95 percent of child sexual assaults are committed by a close family member or friend, and approximately 70 percent of these take place within the home of the victim, close relative, or family friend (Bratina, 2013). This illustrates that the sex predator does not need a public area to prey on their victims.

Over the years, the many high-profile cases that have gained national and international attention have helped to place very high scrutiny on sex offenders, especially child sex offenders. Law enforcement, criminal justice professions, private mental health services, and the politicians who pass laws governing sex offenses are now held to a much higher standard for public safety and reduced recidivism. More restrictions and tougher sentencing is never out of discussion for these offenders. Most politicians publicly support a get-tough approach to sex offenders because it is favorable to the voting public, and no politician wants be accused of being soft on crime, especially when it comes to child predators.

With this intense pressure from the public, law makers continue to support and legislate restrictive conditions on convicted sex offenders that most other released offenders do not have to endure. There are some states, like Indiana, that have a Sex and Violent Offender Registry that includes sex offenders of all classifications and levels and also certain violent offenders who may pose a threat to public safety.

Statement of the Problem

The problem with sex offender residency restrictions is that they restrict or prohibit an individual with a previous sexual criminal history of offenses against children from being within a specified distance (usually between five hundred to two thousand feet) of a school, park, playground, daycare center, or other areas where children may congregate, in hopes that the child sexual predator will not have an opportunity to select a victim in one of these areas (Bratina, 2013). Although there are cases where children are abducted from one of these public areas and sexually assaulted and sometimes murdered by a stranger, the research shows that approximately 95 percent of child sexual assaults are committed by a close family member or friend and does not need a public area to prey on their victims.

The problem is that there are many restrictions

for sex offenders throughout the country that place very restrictive and punitive measures on these individuals in hopes of preventing and deterring sex offenses against children. To date, most research that has been produced on this topic has shown that these restrictions are not likely to increase public safety (Tewksbury, 2011). Many people believe that these measures, if properly enforced, will accomplish that goal. If individuals believe that these restrictions will protect vulnerable children from child sex predators on a large scale of effectiveness, they are sadly mistaken and may be putting their own children at risk.

Even though violent offenders are required to register and have their photos and information about their convictions on the website for all to see, they do not have residency restrictions. So, in many jurisdictions throughout the country, a convicted murderer who is released from prison does not have any residency restrictions placed upon him unless it is a specific condition of probation or parole supervision.

The purpose of this study is to educate society about the dangers of child sex offenders, the residency restrictions that are enforced to prevent and reduce such crimes that in reality have very little or no impact at all, and what can actually be done to effectively address this problem. This study's purpose is also to bring awareness to the fact that many people have a false sense of security, believing their children are only in danger when they are in public or around strangers. Although those dangers do exist—and they will be discussed—the greatest dangers are found within their own close family members and friends.

Conceptual Framework of the Study

This study is framed within the context of examining (1) the locations in which registered sex offenders repeat assaults; (2) whether sex offender residency restrictions that are in force throughout the country reduce recidivism; (3) the reasons therefore; (4) and what further practices can be put in place to minimize reoffending.

Purpose of the Study

This study is designed to examine what can be done to prevent and reduce child sexual assaults.

This information can then be conveyed to society so that families and communities can take action to protect themselves and their children from possible victimization (Bratina, 2013).

The counties responsible for supervising sex offenders also create a sex offender registry that is complete with updated photos, residence addresses, employer names and addresses, and specific sex offenses and classifications, and this is available online for the public to search for offenders in their areas. This is designed for public awareness of these individuals, not public harassment and ridicule.

Research Questions

Based upon the background of the issue and the problem statement, the principal research questions that are addressed are:

1. Do the locations in which registered sex offenders repeat their assaults correlate with sex offender residency restrictions?
2. Do sex offender residency restrictions throughout the country reduce recidivism?

3. What are the reasons the restrictions do or do not work?

4. What further practices can be put in place that would minimize reoffending?

In addition to determining the current restrictions and their effectiveness, the research questions also provide insight and direction into what laws, policies, or procedures would be most effective in reducing and preventing sex offenses against children.

Procedures

In this study, I reviewed literature that addressed the effectiveness of sex offender residency restrictions, management of sex offenders in the community, policy implications, sex offender isolation, and crime prevention theories—to name just a few. For each of these related topics I looked for correlation between effectiveness of residency restrictions for prevention and recidivism reduction. From there, I identified four items of published original research that are relevant to the study and suitable for in-depth analyses. The next step was to establish the criteria for data collection followed by an examination of the selected research for those previously identified criteria.

Significance of the Study

My research is based specifically on articles that have addressed the issue of effectiveness of sex offender residency. Another issue I have looked at is whether or not sex offender residency restrictions create a false sense of security for the general public. If society at large or a specific community are well aware that sex offenders are not allowed at parks or playgrounds, will this influence parents or caregivers to allow young children to play in those areas without their supervision? If they feel a sex offender would not violate this restriction and face severe punishments, are the parents more likely to allow children to play unsupervised away from home? These are questions I will address.

It is now my understanding that sex offender residency restrictions do very little, if anything at all, in the way of deterrence to repeat sexual offenses. According to Huebner et al (2014), the research on child sex victims suggests that the restrictions of residence locations of sex offenders are not likely to achieve their intended goals. The vast majority of sex offenses with children are perpetrated by a close friend or family member, not a stranger.

It would be reasonable to assume that if measures were taken to educate parents and caregivers about research findings, they may then begin to create safer and more protective environments for children, thereby drastically reducing the chances of child sex offenses occurring. It is quite evident from the research that most parents and caregivers of child sex victims do not understand the reality of who is most likely to pose the greatest danger to their children—the acquaintance rather than the stranger.

Another important change should come from the courts. Whenever an individual has been found guilty of a child sex offense, after incarceration has ended and the offender is returned to the community, that person should be prohibited by law from having any access to children under the age of eighteen, including any family members. With current laws in place, child sex offenders may leave prison with restrictions of residency, work, parks, and playgrounds, but unless it's specified by probation or parole departments, these individuals may still have access to children who belong to family and friends. Not all sex offenders have lifetime probation or parole commitments and at some point will be free of supervision and restrictions. Laws need to be changed to prevent any possible access to children.

Residency restrictions may make many people feel a protective barrier is in place for their children. While these restrictions may help to some degree, when access is given to the predator by well-meaning friends or family members, current laws and policies will do very little protect the children and instead create a false sense of security for many in our society.

Limitations of the Study

The analyses of the selected items of research do not take into account how many children are protected from sexual assault by residency restrictions. There is no way of knowing how many children could have been victimized at a park but weren't because the offender obeyed restrictions. The overwhelming majority of child sexual assaults happen at the child's home, the perpetrator's home, or an area that is common and frequented by both the offender and the victim.

This study does not speculate about the number of child sex offenses that may have occurred if a repeat offender violated imposed restrictions. In other words, it's impossible to quantify assaults that did not happen because the offender was not in a restricted location where an assault might have otherwise occurred.

A second limitation of this study is that it only gives data on adult sex offenders and not juvenile sex offenders. There are many cases of juvenile sexual assaults of minor children that are not included in state registries. Many underage individuals molest other children each year, but those are not included in this study. Juvenile sex offenders are not required to register as sex offenders unless they were waived and convicted in an adult court. This allows juvenile sex offenders to live in and visit places that are restricted to adult sex offenders.

Organization of the Thesis

The organization of this study will be structured as (I) the introduction, (II) the literature review, (III) data collection, (IV) data analysis, (V) the conclusion, (VI) appendices, and (VII) tables and figures (if any).

Chapter 2

Literature Review

The research I am undertaking involves questions that surround the following: (1) Do sex offender residence restrictions prevent or reduce sex offenses? (2) Does the location where a sex offender live correlate with sexual assaults? (3) What are the reasons sex offender residence restrictions do or do not work? (4) What would work to reduce or prevent sexual assaults?

The literature review I present specifically surrounds those questions that will show whether sex offender residency restrictions do, in fact, prevent or reduce child sexual victimization and the underlying factors that contribute to it. I will show whether the restrictions provide a false sense of security to the public, and I will show what has been effective in preventing child sex crimes. The literature review will not go into detail analyzing adult sex crime victims, because most sex offender residency restrictions are geared at preventing future child sex crimes.

My argument is that sex offender residency restrictions do not reduce or prevent sexual assaults of child victims, but they do provide a false sense of security that sex offenders will not go to restricted areas where children are likely to congregate. The literature review reveals overwhelming evidence that most child sex victims are not victimized in places where sex offenders are restricted from physically being located.

One area of disagreement remains: whether sex offender residency restrictions actually *increase* the chances that a sex offender will reoffend.

Bratina (2013) has posited that many are now in favor of repealing such restrictions. Investigators, including Danielle Tolosn, Jennifer Klien, and Kelly Socia, have all supported the revamping of current sex offender residence restrictions because of their ineffectiveness to reduce or prevent sex crimes. Research shows that most sex offenses—especially those against children—happen in a home situation with a family member or close family friend. The research shows that current sex offender residence restrictions will not prevent these types of crimes.

As we can see, Tolson and Klein (2015) believe that sex offender residence restrictions can lead to an increase in crime because the separation from family and friends created by these restrictions can add to the pressure of being on the registry and can create a situation in which emotional triggers cause a relapse. We can also see that Bratina (2013), Mustaine (2014), and Huebner et al (2014), take a different view. Based on the evidence presented, it does appear that the undertaking of social isolation and stigmatization produces negative results, which according to Tolson and Klein (2015), may result in predators reoffending.

Some researchers posit that sex offender residence restrictions create negative circumstances that may enhance the chances that a sex offender will reoffend. I simply do not support this view. I do agree that having restrictions on where a person may live can create a hardship in finding suitable housing and work opportunities. Often sex offenders are limited in the areas they can live as to not violate their restrictions. This, in turn, can create an increased number of sex offenders living in relatively close proximity to one another and can limit the opportunity for them to live close to family members, churches, and employment opportunities.

Based upon the results of the research by Bratina (2013), I do not think there is sufficient evidence to support the notion that restricting a sex offender from living in specific areas where children are more likely to congregate is a factor that can increase recidivism. Research shows that most child sex abuse victims are abused by a family member or a close family friend who has access to the child rather than a stranger abusing a child in a public area. Residency restrictions and public notification laws—such as Megan's Law, which requires police officers to notify the public when a high-risk sex offender has moved into the community—are designed to protect the public from child sexual predators (Bratina, 2013). But in reality, these measures do very little to prevent or reduce child sex victims. Bratina's research has revealed that when comparing child sex victimization to adult victimization, approximately 77 percent of child victimization takes place in the home compared to 55 percent of adult victimization. In addition, approximately 95 percent of child victims are victimized by a family member or close family friend. According to Budd (2016), there are no research results that sex offender residence restrictions have a positive influence on recidivism for sex offenses. These statistics show why I disagree with Bratina that residency restrictions can actually increase child sex offenses.

It is true that many sexual-crime recidivism polices are based on the premise that, by notifying the public of where sex offenders are living, this will create a public monitoring of these individuals and keep the public safe (Mustaine, Tewksbury, & Stengel, 2006). This appears to support the effort for citizens to know where sex offenders live and work and to know the classification of their offenses. To say this has no value whatsoever would be incorrect, because if this increases a parent's supervision of their child, it can only produce positive results, and it is possible it could prevent a child from being abducted or sexually abused.

There are cases where children are sexually abused by a neighbor who may be on the lookout for a potential target. If there is increased vigilance in the community because it is known that a sex offender is in their midst, the heightened supervision and security measures may prevent child sex victimization from happening (Mustaine, Tewksbury, & Stengel, 2006). I must support this effort—because even if one child is saved and protected, I cannot see how people would oppose it. The rights of sex offenders and privacy rights will not be covered in this review.

Bratina (2013) proposes that routine activity theory and labelling theory should be applied to combat sex offender recidivism. I will start with the proposition that recidivism can be reduced by understanding the routine activity theory and apply the principles to child sex offenders, although it does describe many of the situations in which children are victimized.

First, the routine activity theory posits that crime is much more likely to occur when variables converge—when you have a motivated offender, a suitable target, and the absence of capable guardians (Bratina, 2013). My research has shown that, since the vast majority of child sex offenses take place in the home and are committed by a relative or family friend (Bratina, 2013), this theory would apply when (1) there is a person who is inclined to desire children as sexual targets (motivated offender), (2) a child is accessible to them (suitable target), and (3) there is an absence of capable guardians (parents not supervising). This is exactly what happens in many victimizations because the offender has access to the family, the home, and the child because of their familial or friendly connection (Bratina, 2013). This does often create the situation for this victimization to occur. In order for a parent or guardian to know the implications of the routine activity theory, they would have to have prior knowledge that the individual who has access to their child is susceptible to committing sexual acts with children. According to Bratina (2013), without this prior knowledge, the parent or guardian quite often does not consider the risks that are created.

Second, in many cases where a family member or family friend has victimized a child sexually, the court will order that the offender can no longer have access to that child, and in many cases cannot be around any children under sixteen years of age, without supervision (R. Pell, personal communication, August, 2019). In this situation, the routine activity theory would not be applicable because the sex offender at this point has been ordered to stay away from the victim(s), and in most cases, the parents or guardians will not allow future contact.

Residency restrictions are designed to take the

opportunity away from the motivated offender so there is no chance he will have the opportunity to commit the act (Mustaine, 2014). This does sound like the routine activity theory is being used to devise plans to take away opportunity from previous offenders. When sex offenders are restricted from being near schools, playgrounds, parks, daycare centers, and school bus stops, it takes away the opportunity for them to look for a suitable target in those areas. According to Bratina (2013), if sex offenders do abide by the restrictions, it is possible that potential recidivism is reduced. It is not possible to know how many repeat offenses are deterred by residency restrictions, but I think it is plausible to consider that there is some amount of deterrence.

I fully support restricting convicted child sex offenders from playgrounds, parks, daycare centers, elementary schools, and school bus stops where children are vulnerable. I believe this can prevent some offenses from happening, but as I stated earlier, it is impossible to know how many potential victims are protected because the sex offender does stay away from such areas. The research therefore does not support removing or reducing these types of restrictions for child predators, but the prevention effect is likely minimal. Most in society do not want to take the chance of putting children at risk over the inconvenience of a sex offender. As I have stated repeatedly, this will not reduce many of the first time offenders who are committing the acts of assault in their homes and in the homes of the children.

Bratina (2013) also believes that labeling theory can have a counter-productive result when sex offenders are well known in their communities. According to Bratina (2013), the negative labels given to sex offenders are more likely to cause them to commit additional deviance or to further become the deviants society believes them to be. This theory posits that the individual will commit more crimes because of the stigmatizing effect the label has on them, and a person who is falsely accused and labeled may now commit the crimes they had not committed in the past.

The author also describes that social control theory presents the premise that people are predisposed to commit crime and that if they lack a close social bond with various elements of society they are more likely to commit crime because they do not have a feeling of connection or obligation to follow society's rules. If a person has a close bond with schools, churches, civic organizations, social organizations, and the ability to build friendships within the community, they are much less likely to commit crimes. So by being labeled as a sex offender, predator, pervert, and criminal, social control theory would support the action that the individual will no longer be an accepted member of the community, and because of this, they will be more likely to reoffend.

A closely related and connected emphasis of labeling theory is that of reintegrative shaming and disintegrative shaming. According to Braithwaite (1989), this is the approach where the offender will experience shaming and condemnation for their actions from family, friends, and members of the community who are expressing their outrage at the offenders' behavior. However, in reintegrative shaming, after the shaming of the offender, all of those involved and the community at large are willing to forgive and reconcile the offender back into the community as a regular member. No further condemnation, shaming, blaming, or punishment is presented. This would allow the offender to have self-worth and possibly become a productive, law-abiding citizen.

In disintegrative shaming, the negative labels ascribed to the offender will remain, and stigmatization of the offender will continue (Braithwaite, 1989). No effort will be made on the part of family, friends, and community to reconcile with the offender, and the offender will be considered an outcast by the community—and by the offender himself. If the offender feels that they are an outcast with no forgiveness or acceptance, the offender will feel no close ties with family, friends, or community, and will be more likely to commit crimes as it is believed in social control theory.

The labeling theory and social control theory both carry some validity in assessing why some offenders may be compelled to commit crimes against others. I do agree with the author's position that when an individual feels more connected to family, friends, and community, they are much more likely to hold a social bond and sense of responsibility in which they would not want to disappoint others. Their desire to maintain a positive position within their families, peer groups, and communities can be a deterrent or control mechanism for many. To be branded as a criminal— and especially as a child sex predator—is one of the worst labels an individual can acquire in our society, and the stigmatizing impact can be devastating for some.

The research of Burchfield (2011), also supports the belief that sex offender residency restrictions do not prevent initial cases of offending and do very little to reduce the chances of repeat offenses. According to Burchfield, polices that have been adopted nationwide are a response to public outcry and the politicians' motivation to gain favor by supporting such policies.

Bratina's and Burchfield's positions that many of these policies have been implemented without any supporting research suggests such polices will reduce or prevent repeat offenses from occurring. In fact, most of the research that has been developed contradicts these policies and restrictions. The residence restrictions often times greatly limit arears where sex offenders can live, creating clusters of areas where there is a high number of sex offenders living in non-restricted areas.

Many of these sex offenders are relegated to socially disorganized neighborhoods with high crime, drugs, gangs, and other incivilities.

According to Burchfield (2011), many sex offenders will be forced to reside in socially disorganized neighborhoods that lack positive social structure and opportunities for sex offender treatment programs. This positon is not unique to Burchfield and is consistent throughout the research on sex offenders living in socially disorganized neighborhoods. The assumed rationale for sex offender residency restrictions and registration requirements is to give the community the knowledge of where sex offenders live and work and to be aware of them (Burchfield, 2011). If sex offenders are forced to live in limited and socially disorganized neighborhoods, it may create a situation where residents are able to watch and communicate with each other about sex offenders in their community.

One of many problems with socially disorganized neighborhoods is that they are transient, and people do not often develop close and trusting relationships with others. This will often be an impediment to residents sharing information about issues in their communities and neighborhoods (Burchfield, 2011). In many of these socially disorganized neighborhoods, where there may be a high number of sex offenders, residents do not know or trust each other and do not participate in community activities. One consequence is a lack of residents who look out for one another—including watching for child sex offenders in their midst. Besides the city issues, sex offenders are also often forced into sparsely populated rural areas where transportation, employment, and available treatment centers aren't easily accessible. This can lead to isolation and less supervision for the offender. This can have negative consequences with the offenders' rehabilitation and reintegration.

From this, Burchfield's position that residence restrictions can actually increase offending appears to be valid. The position is that, if sex offenders are not allowed to return to their home neighborhoods where they have family and possibly better access to work, the hardships that are created by forcing them to live in certain areas can increase enough stress to trigger a relapse (Burchfield, 2011). Their isolation will prohibit, or at least reduce, formal and informal control mechanisms on their behavior. With this position, child sexual predators that are true pedophiles have sexual desires for pre-pubescent children, and that does not subside if they are allowed to return to a familiar living arrangement that they enjoyed before and during the offense(s).

To think that a child sex offender is less likely to offend in a familiar and comfortable city or neighborhood does not sound plausible or rational. Just as is it wrong to think a child sex offender who is forced to live in an area he is not accustomed to or is a socially disorganized neighborhood seems unlikely and is not supported by research. Research does show that crime is much more prevalent in socially disorganized neighborhoods for most criminal offenses, but this does not equate to a disproportionate levels of child sex offending as compared to the heightened levels of various other crimes.

However, Zgoba (2011), also supports the premise that sex offenders more densely occupy socially disorganized neighborhoods, and they would also have more access to unsupervised victims in these areas. Zgoba reaches further by postulating that sex offenders should be restricted from socially disorganized neighborhoods for prevention of future sex crimes as compared to limiting and restricting them from living in other areas that might be more suitable for treatment, rehabilitation, and family.

Most researchers are in agreement that most sex offender residence restrictions do very little to prevent sexual crimes. Even as Zgoba (2011) decries the placement of sex offenders in socially disorganized neighborhoods, she refers to a recent New Jersey study denouncing sex offender registration and notification laws as effective measures to reduce time to first re-arrest or any effect on first time arrests. Once again, this study showed that there is no reduction in first time sex offenses or repeat sex offenses that can be attributed to sex offender notification and registration laws. I do agree with this research because there is no substantive research that has shown a correlation between a sex offender's living location and the increased likelihood that he will commit the first offense or a repeat offense. These restrictions often force sex offenders into areas of high crime.

According to Tewksbury (2011), the use of sex offender residence restrictions will compound registered sex offenders into high-crime, socially disorganized neighborhoods. If this is true, and it appears that most of the research does agree, why do we continue this practice? Unfortunately, the public's false sense of security that has been created by these restrictions and politicians who believe any support or effort made to eliminate or ease such restrictions would become a very controversial and damaging issue for their political careers. No politician wants to be viewed as or described as being soft on criminals— especially criminals who sexually victimize children. Restrictions of residency for living and working are not practical as an approach of criminal justice policy, and it is not a productive means of public safety (Zgoba, 2011). These restrictions and limitations have been shown over and over to not be productive in reducing or preventing crime, and some even claim that it is counter-productive for public safety. I do agree with the many researchers for this first part of this statement; however, I am convinced of their research on the second part.

According to Mustaine (2014), a study in Michigan comparing sex and non-sex offenders discovered that restrictions of residence for sex offenders had very little influence on sex offender recidivism, and sex offenders are slightly more likely to recidivate than non-sex offenders. I agree with these findings as well. Child sex offenders are more likely to recidivate than many non-sex offender classifications, and the sex offender residency restrictions placed upon them is doing very little—if anything at all—to prevent it.

I also agree with Mustaine, and contrary to some other researchers, she also proposes that sex offender residency restrictions have been shown at the macro level will not increase rates of child sex victimization. Furthermore, she has also found that, because of the restrictions, many sex offenders are forced to live in very socially disorganized neighborhoods that lack social efficacy, employment opportunities, adequate housing, and opportunities for treatment. These neighborhoods are very high crime areas, gang ridden, have high rates of rudeness and incivilities, and lack community cohesion. They do not foster a sense of community for individuals who are new to the area to feel welcomed. It is these conditions that create a feeling of isolation for many sex offenders. Those factors alone can create conditions where many people are more susceptible to criminal behavior.

Conclusion

Most of the research analyzing sex offender residency restrictions are in agreement that these restrictions do not prevent initial cases of sexual victimization, nor do they reduce recidivism of sex offenders (Bratina, 2013). This is especially true with child sexual victimization. The vast majority of the cases of child sexual victimization are perpetrated by a family member of a close family friend. These people are trusted individuals who have access to the child's home, often even having the ability to take the child away from the home. These are hidden dangers that sex offender residency restrictions cannot foresee or prevent.

There are cases where children are abducted in a public place that is restricted to sex offenders, but that is a small percentage compared to the victimizations that take place in non-restricted areas. This is not to lessen the impact of the cruelty and trauma to the victim and the family, and any child who is protected by such laws make the inconvenience to sex offenders worth it, in my opinion. However, citizens should not develop a false sense of security in believing that all sex offender restricted areas are sex offender free. They are not free of child sexual predators.

Residency restrictions often limit sex offenders to socially disorganized neighborhoods that are high-crime areas (Tewksbury, 2011). Many of these neighborhoods do not provide adequate housing, employment opportunities, or close proximity to family members. They also do not possess adequate treatment options. Many of these neighborhoods do provide crime opportunities, stress, isolation, lack of opportunity, and—some say—the conditions that may trigger sexual offending.

In conclusion, the major findings of the studies that I have presented have been very consistent with their results. Sex Offender residence restrictions do very little, if anything at all, to prevent sexual assaults or reduce recidivism for sexual offenders. Sex offender residence restrictions do create a false sense of security for many in the general public who are unaware of where research tells us sex offenses are most likely to happen. Sex offenses are most likely to happen in places where sex offender restrictions do not apply.

Chapter 3

Data Collection and Analysis

Introduction

In this chapter, I present the data collection and analysis used in this study. I begin with the methodology employed in order to select the most appropriate and applicable published between them, the research questions, and the criteria for selection. The question I have elected is: Do sex offender residency restrictions prevent or reduce sex offenses against children, or do they provide a false sense of security? Finally, I discuss the analysis of each of the research items from the perspectives of textual analysis, the research context, methods used, and results.

Methodology

In order to select the published articles that present the best opportunity to effectively address my research questions, I developed a set of criteria. These criteria are set out here:

(a) Do the research articles address public perception of sex offender residency restrictions and their effectiveness?

(b) Do the research articles provide statistical evidence of reduced sexual offenses of children due to the effectiveness of the restrictions?

(c) Do the research articles provide evidence explicating where child sex offenses are most likely to occur?

Data Collection

Using the criteria set out in the methodology section, I undertook an in-depth search of applicable databases to find a variety of scholarly research in this area. As a result, I selected the following items of published research for analysis.

I selected the research undertaken by Kristen Budd, entitled, "Crime Control Theatre: Public (Mis) Perceptions of Effectiveness of Sex Offender Residence Restrictions," and published by *Psychology, Public Policy, and Law*. My initial review indicates that it will have substantive value to the research questions I have presented for researching. The researcher addresses several of the criteria set out in my methodology, which are (1) do sex offender residence restrictions reduce or prevent sexual assaults and especially assaults of child victims?, and (2) do sex offender residence restrictions provide a false sense of security? The effectiveness of sex offender residence restrictions and why they are not effective and if the public has a false sense of security regarding their effectiveness. According to the author, with the dramatic increase of public concern over sex offenses perpetrated on children, this has perpetuated a heightened increase of law-makers.

For this reason, the findings of Budd's research help to address two of my research questions: Do sex offender residence restrictions reduce or prevent child sex offenses?; and do sex offender residence restrictions produce a false sense of security that their children are not in danger of being sexually assaulted? And the research has produced findings that do not support any crime reduction due to their enforcement.

The second item of published research I selected, "Examining the Correlates of Sex Offender Residence Restriction Violation Rates," which was published by the *Journal of Quantitative Criminology* in 2017, produced supporting results. In this article, Jason Rydberg, Eric Grommon, Beth Huebner, and Breanne Pleggenkuhle produced results from the research that supports the belief that sex offender residence restrictions do not prevent crime or reduce sexual recidivism.

The third published research article I selected that addressed the criteria was, "Making Sense out of Nonsense: The deconstruction of State-Level Sex Offender Residence Restrictions," published by the *American Journal of Criminal Justice* in 2008. In this research study, the investigators of Michelle Meloy, Susan Miller, and Kristin Curtis sought to illustrate that data prove sex offender residence restrictions are driven by fear and not from the results of empirical evidence. The authors of the article clearly show that sex offender residence restrictions do very little to prevent or reduce sex crimes.

The fourth published research article I selected addresses criteria A and B that I have chosen for my study. The article, "Sex Offender Residency Requirements: An Effective Crime Prevention strategy or A False Sense of Security?" was published by the *Journal of Police Science & Management*, in 2013. I selected this article because it does answer the three criteria I have selected for my study. The researcher of this study, Michele Bratina, has produced findings that clearly illuminate the facts pertaining to sex offender residence restrictions. Her findings show that sex offender residence restrictions do not reduce or prevent sex crimes; it shows that most child sexual assault cases happen in the child's home or the home of a relative or close family friend; and finally, that current sex offender laws create a false sense of security of their effectiveness.

The studies address the criteria I have established by providing evidence from research that answers my questions of (1) do sex offender residence restrictions prevent or reduce sexual assaults and especially of child victims, and (2) do sex offender residence restrictions create a false sense of security for the public. These studies, as well as others I have researched, each address the research questions I pose and each clearly and convincingly provide evidence through sound research that answers these questions.

Each of the studies presented in this section provides clear findings of data that are used to address the criteria I have established. Some of the studies address more than one of the criteria I have established and one of them only addresses one of the criteria. Additionally, much of the research findings established in each of these studies are very consistent with each of the other studies and are complimentary of each other.

Data Analysis

Introduction

The research was conducted by Kristen M. Budd of Miami University and Christina Mancini of Virginia Commonwealth University. Their interest in producing the research study was to illustrate the ineffectiveness of sex offender residence restrictions and the public's misperceptions of them. The research was conducted in 2016, with Budd's research being conducted at the University of Miami and Mancini's research being conducted at the Virginia Commonwealth University.

The research was conducted to dispel myths about sex offender residence restrictions concerning their effectiveness and the misperceptions of them. The study was focused on sex offender residence restrictions within the United States and did not provide or produce any evidence of research from outside the United States. The question posed by the researchers was relevant to the production of evidence illustrated that sex offender residence restrictions do not reduce or prevent child sexual victimization.

Study 1: Crime Control Theatre: Public (Mis) Perceptions of the Effectiveness of Sex Offender Residence Restrictions. Budd, K.M., & Mancini, C. (2016). *Psychology, Public Policy, and Law, 22(4),* 362-374.

Analysis

The statement of purpose in the article emphasizes the position of the authors that it is their belief from their research findings that many in the public have a misguided confidence in the effectiveness of sex offender residence restrictions.

The authors of this study provide a very clear and coherent sequence of questions and research results that allow the readers to understand how sex offender residence restrictions are created, how they are supported by public fear, and their actual level of effectiveness. The investigators of this study focused on evidence that would cosign findings that would clearly show that there are misperceptions of sex offender residence restrictions about their effectiveness and their perceived effectiveness by the public. Both of which are problematic when the prevention of sexual assaults and child victimization are the focus.

According to Budd and Mancini, the use of residence restrictions is an element of the Crime Control Theatre, which posits that these laws are created and supported by moral panic that is unsubstantiated. Furthermore, the authors also present the evidence of the public's unquestioned acceptance of sex offender residence restrictions and high support of the laws and the "stranger danger" belief is more likely to contribute to child sexual assaults than relatives or close family friends.

Methods

The methods utilized in this study were sound, accurate, and practical. The methods are valid for studying this problem with the use of dependent variables, independent variables, and controlled variables. According to the authors of the study, the dependent variable measures the perceived effectiveness of the residence restrictions by the public and their ability to decrease the likelihood that sex offenders will commit new crimes. The independent variables measured the source of information that most in the public acquire their information about sex offenders and especially the different types of media that may influence the moral panic process.

A thorough review of the data provided in the tables finds that the statistics presented are sound and accurate. Information provided from surveys revealing public opinion was used from experts in the field studying sex offenses. Several data sources were used that are specifically designed to review the public's opinion of the effectiveness of sex offender residence restrictions. The title of the legend accurately describes and illustrates the information that supports the findings of sex offender residence restrictions effectiveness. The results that are presented in the tables repeat some of the information from the text; however, there is much more added information in the tables that not only supports the text, but adds substantial breakdowns and categories of critical information.

The surveys used contained questions that were designed to illicit the opinions and expressed faith in the effectiveness of the criminal justice system's ability to monitor and supervise sex offenders through a variety of processes and the use of sex offender residence restriction laws. The methods also provided professional sourced information that was retrieved from probation and parole departments, community corrections, and victim notification systems.

After an exhaustive review of the data, the calculations that are provided are sound and accurate and support what the researchers are intending to substantiate. I find the study to be of extreme value because the information and methods used were accurate and substantial. This information came from accurate reporting by professional criminal justice agencies and sound research methods. From this study, the findings clearly show that sex offender residence restrictions do not reduce or prevent sexual assaults, despite public perception that they do.

Results

The various tables presented in the study provide in-depth statistics on perceptions of sex offender residence restrictions, primary source information concerning sex offenders, the characteristics of sex crimes victims, and the relationship between victims and offenders. This information provides a clear and succinct illustration of the characteristics of sex crimes and the public's opinion about them.

The tables align succinctly with the title of the research article and the information provided within the text. The tables provide considerable amounts of statistics that are not detailed within the text of the article. It does however supplement the information that is provided within the text.

Discussion

The discussion for the study is a basic summation of the content of the text. It does not provide any new information or findings and merely echoes the theme of the study. The discussion admits to a few limitations, such as age demographics and educational attainment among those studied. This does not, however—in the author's and my opinion—skew the findings that address the research question and the results of the study overwhelmingly address and answer the question posed.

The study does consider many key studies in this filed that either directly or indirectly address this issue and the questions posed. These studies do have very similar results and help to coalesce a body of knowledge indicating that sex offender residence restrictions do not reduce or prevent sexual assaults and they do in fact create a false sense of security for their perceived effectiveness for the public.

The study supports and recommends that additional and more in-depth research should be conducted in the areas of laws that target sex crimes and their popularity among the public.

Significance of the Research and Conclusions

The significance of the study is an important one because it illustrates that many in the general public have the belief that children are most often sexually assaulted from a "stranger danger" situation and if tough residence restrictions are adhered to, children— and even adults—will be protected from sexual assaults. The study shows that is not true. The study does show that many in the general public believe these restrictions are essential for preventing sexual assaults.

The supporting research studies cited were not in contradiction to the authors of this study and were very supportive of the claims put forth by the researchers. The study does suggest that more research needs to be conducted concerning the laws that are driven by moral panic or politicians who do not want to appear soft on crime—especially sexual predators. These recommendations suggest that laws can be used to address sex offenders in a way that are productive and not merely an overreaction to public cries for tougher, more restrictive, and punitive laws.

I find this study to be very informative because it produces a thorough analysis of the public's perception and knowledge of sex offender laws and the statistics of sex offense patterns. This is extremely helpful in understanding why so many argue for more punitive and restrictive sex offender residence restrictions even though the research contradicts much of what they believe and support. This study illustrates the need for the dissemination of facts to politicians, criminal justice professionals, and to the general public, so that laws can be based on facts and evidence, not emotion.

Study 2: Examining the Correlates of Sex Offender Residence Restriction Violation Rates. Rydberg, J., Grommon, E., Huebner, B., & Pleggenkuhle, B. (2017). *Journal of Quantitative Criminology, 33(2)*, 347-369.

Introduction

The study was conducted by Jason Rydberg, Eric Grommon, Beth Huebner, and Breanne Pleggenkuhle. The research was conducted at the University of Massachusetts Lowell, Indiana University-Purdue University of Indianapolis, the University of Missouri-St. Louis, and Southern Illinois University and published in 2017.

The research was conducted to show contribution of factors to sex offending and the differences in violation rates around or in sex offender restricted areas. Specific attention is given to social and ecological factors that contribute to sex offender violation rates. The study does show a correlation between sex offenses and the density of offenders living in areas where they are not in violation of distance laws. The study shows that restricting sex offenders from living in certain areas of a community and limiting their housing opportunities to certain disadvantaged neighborhoods may actually increase sex offending and accelerate recidivism.

The study did not seek any findings on an international or national level, but rather pulled from two Midwestern states for its conclusions. The research was based on the position that sex offender residence restrictions have been widely used for over twenty years in an attempt to prevent and reduce sex offenses in communities. There was no indication that the research was influenced by funding mechanisms or specific allocations for a specific topic of research. Instead, this study was conducted by the intense desire of the authors.

Analysis

The statement of purpose of the study and the objective of the study were to show that sex offender populations that commit sexual offenses and repeat offenses are not discouraged or prohibited from committing these acts due to established sex offender residence restrictions. The statement of purpose is closely aligned with the stated subject addressed in the abstract and builds upon it through the text. The introduction details a limited scope of the overall research study and gives a narrowly defined description that is much less in depth than what is presented later in the text. In this article, the investigator dissects the contribution of social factors to the fluctuation in sex offender residence restriction violation rates, practical as a sex offender living within a restricted zone around a school, daycare, or other prohibited area.

Furthermore, the analysis reveals that conditions discovered to be associated with sex offender clustering are not linked with sex offender residence restriction violation rates.

Methods

The methods that were used for this study were appropriate and valid for the study of this issue because the data that was used scientifically illustrated the lack of effectiveness of sex offender residence restrictions and their ability to reduce or prevent sex crimes. The data compiled was statistically accurate and measureable. This study can be duplicated by other researchers by using the same approach to ascertain similar information that will yield supporting evidence to the authors of this study. Sample selections were gathered from the states of Michigan and Missouri, with thousands of sex offenders represented. This study undertook the examination of county-level sex offender residence restrictions and parolees who violated these restrictions of housing areas, working areas, and the visiting of restricted areas such as playgrounds, parks, daycare centers, and schools.

The methods secured the violation rates of four categories of offenders: (1) pre-sex offender residence restriction, (2) post-sex offender residence restriction, (3) pre-sex offender residence restriction non-sex, and (4) post-sex offender residence restriction non-sex. The categories generated information of sex offenses committed in restricted areas and non-restricted areas by both sex offender parolees and non-sex offender parolees. The data provided for this article was conducted through quantitative research that revealed statistics that show where individuals live before and after a sexual assault did not have any impact on sexual offending. The research shows through the quantitative research that the types of sexual offenses and the characteristics of the victims are not affected by the physical residence of the offender. In the quantitative research method used for this study, descriptive statistics were used to show proportionately of the crimes being committed and also the percentages of different locations for sex offenses. This is extremely useful in illustrating that the belief that sex offender residence restrictions from certain geographic locations can reduce or prevent sexual offenses is not accurate.

The information presented is sequential, detailed, and thorough. This was accomplished by showing the process in which a sex offender who is released from prison and is relegated to live in a socially disorganized neighborhood is more likely to reoffend than those who return to past living conditions. The study also defines such contributing factors as restriction density, higher ex-offender population, and illegal substance availability. This was a consistent finding across all cohorts that were analyzed in this study.

The information is extremely pertinent to the study because of the profound knowledge that is presented to be used for possible future study, practice, and legislation. The results of this study clearly demonstrate, through the use of collected and accurate data, that current sex offender residence restrictions do not reduce or prevent sexual offending.

Results

There are six different tables and diagrams presented in the study that accurately detail and illustrate the findings that support the author's position and recommendation. The information detailed in the tables far surpasses the information given in the text. The tables' statistics and information greatly support and enhance the position of the authors.

The table's present information illustrating the

density of sex offenders in certain geographic areas because they do not fall within a sex offender residence restricted area. Because of this, these areas often become inundated with sex offenders in an already socially disorganized and disadvantaged neighborhood that has an elevated crime rate, poverty rate, unemployment rate, and less opportunity in almost every area for social, economic, and rehabilitative success.

The concentrated areas of sex offenders combined with a disproportionate number of other criminal classifications correlates with higher crime rates across the board and an increased sexual crime rate. The tables show that areas where many sex offenders are relegated to live encounter fewer affordable housing opportunities and higher unemployment rates and are transitional neighborhoods that are socially disorganized. All of these characteristics are associated with higher rates of crime and sexual offenses. Furthermore, these are not the areas many sex offenders resided in when they committed their first sex offense—especially in the case of child sexual predators.

The results of the study present findings that clearly

suggest sex offender residence restrictions do very little, if anything at all, to reduce or prevent sexual assaults of adults or children. The study produces evidence that it may be counter-productive to restrict sex offenders from certain locations because of the density effect that may actually lead to an increase in crime.

I did not detect any discrepancies between the results in the text and what is presented in the tables— only more in-depth statistics. The calculations that are presented in the text and the calculations presented in the tables are in sync. In each presentation within the study, the numbers and information that was compiled undoubtedly demonstrated that sex offender residence restrictions do not reduce or prevent sex crimes and may actually increase it.

Discussion

The interpretation of the data is clear. Overwhelming evidence has been produced to show that sex offender residence restrictions do not reduce or prevent repeat sexual assaults. Furthermore, the study also supports the belief of many individuals in the general public believe are effective in purpose; however, a substantial body of supportive research is cited in the study and lends major credibility and validity to this study that current sex offender residence restrictions do not work as professed. For example, the study "Residence Restriction Buffer Zones and the Banishment of Sex Offenders," by Kristen Zgoba, provides supporting evidence to my selected studies and criteria. Another supporting article is "Sex Offender Residency Restrictions: Successful Integration or Exclusion?" by Elizabeth Mustaine.

The researchers recommend future investigations that aim to replicate this study in order to confirm these findings. Moreover, the authors recommend future investigations to extend beyond the scope of this particular study. For example, further research should be conducted on areas where sex offenders tend to live in large numbers due to their restrictions from many areas of a community. Some research findings, such as in the article "The Prevalence and Correlates of Depression Among Sex Offenders Subject to Community Notification and Residence Restriction Legislation," by Elizabeth Jeglic, Cynthia Calkins, and Jill Levenson, suggest that the limiting of potential housing opportunities may actually lead to increased criminal activity.

Significance of the Research and Conclusion

This research has meaningful implications as to the limitations of housing opportunities for sex offenders and their pseudo-segregation to socially disorganized neighborhoods. Many of these neighborhoods encompass higher rates of crime in almost every category and may even contribute to increased recidivism for sex offenders. The limitations of job opportunities, housing, treatment programs, and the influence of a high criminal element may influence higher crime rates.

The study is very strong in comparing areas where there are high concentrations of sex offenders living in areas where they do not violate the sex offender residence restrictions and the higher rates of criminal activity in such areas. This study also promotes the claim that sex offender residence restrictions do not reduce or prevent sexual assaults, especially with children, because the vast majority of cases are perpetrated by a family member or close family friend in a home that is not restricted from the offender.

The research did not produce any new findings concerning these areas of discussion; however, it is powerful, academically produced evidence that can help determine the validity and usefulness of sex offender residence restrictions that has already been proclaimed in other research articles. I do consider this research to have significant value to academics, law makers, and criminal justice professionals who are involved in implementing meaningful and effective laws and policies that will produce the outcomes that are stated, not laws that simply satisfy public demand and political dictates.

Study 3: Sex Offender Residency Requirements: An Effective Crime Prevention Strategy or a False Sense of Security? Bratina, M.P. (2013). *Journal of Police Science & Management, 15(3),* 200-218.

Introduction

The study was conducted by Michele Bratina of Shippensburg University in Shippensburg,

Pennsylvania in 2013. The author conducted the study with the intent to present findings on the effectiveness of sex offender residence restrictions with a thorough review of most up-to-date empirical research and current literature on this topic. The research was conducted to review findings of similarly designed research to help create evidence that will assist politicians, law makers, and criminal justice professions in establishing evidence-based practices for the supervision and restriction of sex offenders.

The study's research does not only contain information about the author's location, but covers many areas of the United States. Additionally, the study has global ramifications because the study also addresses the issue of child sex tourism that many individuals engage in around the world, including Americans who will travel to foreign countries to have sex with children.

No information was given concerning funding costs or funding sources for the study. The study was based on prior information of sex offender residence restrictions being common across the country, with very specific and similar restrictions for sex offenders on where they can live, work, and visit. The study is based on the assumption that most current sex offender residence restrictions do very little, if anything at all, to prevent or reduce sex assaults, especially those involving child victims.

Analysis

The statement purpose of the study was to address the effectiveness of sex offender residence restrictions in their design to reduce or prevent sex crimes. The title of the paper is addressed throughout the paper, with all cited research focused on answering the questions of sex offenders residence restrictions effectiveness and whether they create a false sense of security. The statement of purpose in the abstract is aligned with the introduction of the study, which informs the reader of the questions that are posed and the research findings that will answer those questions.

Methods

The various methods used for the study are sound and practical and produce clear answers to the questions posed. Findings from many different studies, with various study designs, were analyzed that created a foundation of information that specifically addresses the effectiveness if sex offender residence restrictions.

The first method used was a summation of data from empirical studies used to analyze the impact of collateral consequences of sex offender residence restrictions on sex offenders' reintegration into society. The adverse consequences attached with the label of being a sex offender can create challenges and obstacles that can prevent successful reintegration back into society and can create conditions that lead to increased recidivism. The collateral consequence of having to move to a socially disorganized neighborhood is associated with higher crime rates and higher rates of recidivism. Research shows that because of sex offender residence restrictions that greatly limit where these individuals can live and work, many are relegated to the worst neighborhoods in a community that are socially disorganized, transient, poverty ridden, and crime filled. All are correlated with higher crime rates and higher recidivism.

Secondly, the methods evaluate the impact of

recidivism and spatial analysis. According to the author, the findings of most research studies indicate that sex offenders are not affected by residence restrictions and they are not a mechanism for reducing sex offender recidivism. According to the author, the spatial distances that sex offender residence restrictions place on some offenders place them in a very desolate area that is void of job opportunities, family, and treatment programs. This method of data collection is clearly represented in the tables and gives a clear picture of the collateral consequences of sex offender residence restrictions.

I did not detect any defects from the methods used for collecting and analyzing the data. There were no experimental methods used in the study, only empirical research already produced by leading academics in the field.

The sequence of statements in the methods was practical and linear, which made it easy to follow and process. They allowed the reader to follow the progression of the idea and how it would help lead to a logical and more-informed conclusion. All of the information provided was essential and relevant to the purpose of the study.

Results

There were two tables presented in the study that were helpful in illustrating the significance of cited research publication and the value of their findings and support in this study. The data is clearly organized, which allows for easy comparison, interpretation, and processing of the information so that it can be easily understood in its support of the current study.

Much of the data in the tables is also presented in the text and is repeated in some of the columns. However, there is additional information presented in the tables that is not presented in the text. Some of it is a continuation of information in the text, and some is new information that is supporting in nature. The tables illustrated the limitations of current sex offender residence restrictions and the consequences of spatial observance.

The results of the study strongly support the stated objectives of the author. The information and findings she presents overwhelmingly answers the question posed in the introduction of the study. It is without reservation that I state the research produced in the study strongly supports the proposition that sex offender residence restrictions do not prevent or reduce sexual offenses among all categories of victims—especially child victims.

Discussion

The interpretation of the data does repeat the results of the findings that are paramount to the purpose of the study. The findings are repeated, but not in a simple repeating of the data. It is presented through different explanations, but the result is the same interpretation. Additionally, the study did produce some new questions. The most profound new question is not whether or not sex offender residence restrictions reduce or prevent crime, but alternatively, whether they actually increase other categories of crime from sex offenders due to the collateral negative consequences of the labeling of sex offenders and the restrictions imposed.

The author's position is one that clearly illustrates that current restrictions on sex offenders' living and working locations do not reduce or prevent sexual offenses, and consequently, because of some offenders being forced into socially disorganized neighborhoods, many of them may in fact increase their criminal activity. Additionally, the author posits that may sex offenders are placed in desolate areas with limited housing and job opportunities and little to no treatment options, all which could lead to higher recidivism.

The research study is supported by many other cited sources of academically produced findings. Studies that posed the same or very similar consequences concerning sexual assault victims and the sex offenders were also referenced in the study.

Significance of the Research

The research study is successful due to its conglomeration of significant studies that address the specific question posed by the author and also commensurate with the factors impacting sexual assaults and reducing recidivism. And at least one new question was posed as a result of the study.

The question raised in the study concerned

collateral consequences of the labeling of sex offenders and the limitations of housing opportunities due to the stringent sex offender residence restriction guidelines. Many sex offenders are restricted from living or working with one thousand feet of a school, park, playground, child daycare center, and so forth, and these can be located virtually everywhere throughout a community. This often creates a large concentration of sex offenders into geographically approved areas that are quite often socially disorganized neighborhoods. The author poses the questions and encourages new research on the collateral consequences of the restrictions and correlations of increased criminal activity.

In brief, I feel the study did make a significant contribution to human knowledge on this subject with its clear findings that sex offender residence restrictions do not reduce or prevent sexual assaults of any category of victim and especially child victims. Furthermore, with its findings there is the hypothesis that the restrictive nature of sex offender residence restrictions that they may actually increase crime in certain situations.

Study 4: Making Sense out of Nonsense: The Deconstruction of State-Level Offender Residence Restrictions. Meloy, M.L. Miller, S.L., & Curtis, K.M. (2008). *American Journal of Criminal Justice, 33(2)*, 209-222.

Introduction

The study was conducted by Michelle L. Meloy of Rutgers University, Susan L. Miller of the University of Delaware, and Kristin M. Curtis of Rutgers University. The authors' interest in the study was to show that sex offender residence restrictions, although well-intentioned, do not reduce or prevent sexual assaults or child molestations.

The study was not exclusive to only the states of the authors, but rather, it considered data from all over the United States. There is valuable data collected, analyzed, and provided from all fifty states for the study. There was no data collected or provided from international locations. There was no information provided on the amount of funding needed, funding sources, or influences other than the authors' desire to answer the question posed for the furthering of knowledge in this area.

The question posed by the researcher is of profound significance. The study addresses the reasons for implementation of sex offender residence restrictions and if they do in fact deliver the quality of effectiveness they are purported and designed to.

Analysis

The objective of the study was to determine if sex offender residence restrictions do, in fact, produce the desired results they are intended and professed to accomplish. The title of the paper does not precisely describe the entirety of what the study encompasses; however, it does give a clear description of a portion of this topic that is significant to addressing it in its entirety.

Methods

The methods used for the study were sound and valid. At least three independent sources were used to validate each entry. The methods used to produce the findings in the study could be replicated in future studies. The sample selection was substantial and adequate as it contained data from all fifty states, and I do not see any flaws in their collection and presentation of the data and how it addresses the questions that they intended to answer.

One of the methods used was to collect and analyze empirical data that is used to justify residence restrictions. However, as the research shows, most of the reasons that are used to implement and justify sex offender residence restrictions are in opposition to the empirical data. The data show that sex offender residence restrictions do very little to curb sex offenses.

The method of collecting findings from three research projects focused on the physical distance of sex offender living locations and the likelihood of reoffending. The data show that spatial distance has little to do with sexual offenses.

As in other studies, the author exposes the potential collateral consequences of sex offender residence restrictions through her method of analyzing additional studies of this nature. The methods provided information that was crucial to addressing the foremost issue of whether sex offender residence restrictions reduce or prevent sex crimes and also the underlying issue of whether they actually increase criminal activity in specific situations.

The method of collecting data that show the prohibited distance from a specific area in relation to the severity of the offense was of a major importance. The data revealed that the prohibited distance from a specific area (as little as five hundred feet and as much as two thousand feet) did not have any impact on the recidivism rate for sex offenders. Additionally, the study revealed that most sex offender residence restrictions are applied to adult sex offenders and not to juvenile sex offenders who may still have access to parks, playgrounds, daycare centers, and so forth.

Results

The data presented in the tables gives information on all states with sex offender residence restrictions and their various distances from prohibited areas and the descriptions of the prohibited areas. The title of the tables accurately describes the content and its relevance to the study.

The data presented in the tables are much more detailed and more descriptive than what is in the text. The text is saturated with data collections and their place in the study, which provides essential and critical information for the validity of the study. The data provided in the tables gives the reader the luxury of easily comparing the findings from each state on their respective sex offender residence restrictions without turning through numerous pages of texts for comparisons.

The comparisons of data presented in the tables to the data presented throughout the text illustrate a matching of those data. There is more data per state provided in the tables that is not entirely disseminated throughout the text. All of the data presented in the text is represented in the tables, but all of the data in the tables is not necessarily represented in the text.

The intentions of the authors is obvious and powerful from the collaboration of questions posed, data collected, and the appropriate application of the data to the questions. It is clear that the authors provided a clear answer to the questions posed.

Discussion

The results provided are clear and without question. Not that they are 100 percent accurate, but they do strongly and overwhelmingly show that, in the vast majority of sex crimes, sex offender residence restrictions had virtually no impact in preventing or reducing them.

The study did express the lack of research and evidence on juvenile sex offenders as compared to adult sex offenders, even if the juvenile sex offender had a child victim. Most of the research on sex offenders and residence restrictions address the issues associated with adult sex offenders leaving an entirely separate group of sex offenders with predominately child victims with very little scrutiny, supervision, and restrictions as compared to adult sex offenders.

The authors strongly encourage the development and implementation of evidence-based policies that will provide the best deterrent and protection for potential sexual assault victims. This should be initiated with an accurate assessment of misperceptions of sex offenders, sex offender laws, and their victims.

Significance of the Research and Conclusions

The research does not yield any new questions concerning sex offender residence restrictions that have not already been asked. However, the study does strongly encourage the review of academic research in this area and recommends that evidence-based practices guide the laws and procedures for the monitoring of sex offenders.

The study has produced, much like the cited research, the overwhelming results that sex offender residence restrictions do very little, if anything at all, to reduce or prevent sex crimes and that a serious revamping of such laws throughout the country, aided by research and evidence-based practices, would lend the best conditions for public safety and monitoring of sex offenders.

Conclusion

Based upon the in-depth analysis and evaluation of the selected items of published research, I have presented strong evidence that addresses my research questions. The evidence conferred from my research concludes with the findings that sex offender residence restrictions do very little to prevent or reduce sexual offenses.

My criteria consisted of three questions: (1) Do the research articles address public perception of sex offender residency restrictions and their effectiveness? (2) Do the research articles provide statistical evidence of reduced sexual offenses of children due to the effectiveness of the restrictions? And (3) Do the research articles provide evidence illustrating where child sex offenses are most likely to occur? Each of the four articles answered all three of the research questions, either in whole or in part, with clear and convincing evidence.

The evidence, comprised of research, produced clear and convincing conclusions that sex offender residence restrictions do very little to reduce or prevent sexual assaults—especially sex offenses against children. Furthermore, the conclusions also accurately depict a public who has more belief if their effectiveness than what research indicates.

Chapter 4

Conclusions and Recommendations

Introduction

Conclusions

Overall, based on the evidence that I have presented from the four research studies, it is clear that sex offender residence restrictions (1) do not reduce or prevent sexual assaults, (2) do provide a false sense of security for many, and (3) have shown that sex offenses against children are less likely to be committed in public or by a stranger.

For example, in the article "Crime Control Theatre: Public (Mis)Perception of the Effectiveness of Sex Offender Residence Restrictions," it is reported that the majority of the general public believes sex offender residence restrictions prevent sexual predators from being in certain public places and that this prevents or reduces many cases of sexual assault. As the investigators accurately posit, this is not true.

The authors of this study accurately present evidence that sex offender residence restrictions do not reduce or prevent sexual offenses, because the majority of the crimes occur in places where sex offenders are not prohibited. Finally, this article dispels the myth that most children are victimized sexually by a stranger, because most child sex offenses are committed by a relative or close family friend who has access to the child.

In the second study, I was exposed to evidence that answered my three research questions. In the article "Examining the Correlates of Sex Offender Residence Restriction Violation Rates," the authors presented evidence that moral panic has helped push and support sex offender restrictions that do not produce the protection many believe it provides.

In this article, the presenters show where the public supports a "stranger danger" approach to protect individuals, especially children, from sexual assault. This approach ignores the evidence that clearly demonstrates that most sexual assaults (both adult and child) are committed by someone known to the victim.

. The investigators of this study focused on evidence that would produce findings that would clearly show there are misperceptions of sex offender residence restrictions—about their real and perceived effectiveness. Both are problematic when the prevention of sexual assaults and child victimization are the focus.

In the third article, I found the author presented evidence that clearly addressed my research questions concerning sex offender residence restrictions creating a false sense of security. In "Sex Offender Residency Requirements: Strategy or a False Sense of Security?" the author provides quantitative data that are overwhelmingly convincing that sex offender residence restrictions do, indeed, create a false sense of security. Again, like the other studies I have analyzed, the author's analysis of this question reveals that many in the general public believe that strict restrictions coupled with severe penalties of sex offenders will reduce or prevent sexual offenses.

The author's position in the study clearly illustrates that current restrictions on sex offenders' living and working locations do not reduce or prevent sexual offenses, and consequently, because of some offenders being forced into socially disorganized neighborhoods, many of them may in fact increase their criminal activity. Additionally, the author contends that many sex offenders are placed in isolated areas with limited housing opportunities and job opportunities and few or no treatment options, all of which could lead to higher recidivism.

Finally, in the article, "Making Sense out of Nonsense: The Deconstruction of State-Level Sex Offender Residence Restrictions," evidence is presented that shows sex offender residence restrictions, no matter their distance variations, do not reduce or prevent sexual offenses. According to the author, sex offender residence restrictions continue to increase in numbers and with support of the public, regardless of the fact that there is no empirical evidence to support the belief.

This article presents evidence that most sexual offenses are committed by someone known to the victim, that they usually take place in an area that would not normally be prohibited to the offender, and that forcing many sex offenders into socially disorganized neighborhoods may contribute to increased criminal activity.

In sum, each of these studies I have presented give clear and convincing evidence that sex offender restrictions do not reduce or prevent sexual offenses, and that most sex offenses are committed by someone known to the victim. In cases involving children, the vast majorities of sex offenders are a family member or close family friend who has access to the child and is not restricted by law from being near them.

Recommendations

After a careful analysis of the various research studies I have presented, I am of the firm conclusion that sex offender residence restrictions do not reduce or prevent sexual assaults from occurring. The laws that are enacted and the enforcement of sex offender residence restrictions should be reassessed after these studies have produced convincing evidence that they do not work as intended.

It is my recommendation that the legislators, prosecutors, and judges review these findings and produce more effective ways of punishment, prevention, and rehabilitation of sex offenders. Protection of children from repeat victimization and protection of all children by stringent restrictions from contact with minor children in any place, especially the children's home and the sex offender's home, would do more to protect children than current sex offender residence restrictions.

Restricting identified sex offenders from being near any underage children they might normally have access to would prevent and reduce most of the sex offenses against children. Current sex offender residence restrictions only restrict offenders where they can live, work, and public places they may visit. Other than a court-ordered or parole-ordered restriction, sex offenders can still visit the homes of children, and children can visit their homes as well. If true protection is to be pursued, then restriction of contact with underage children must be enforced long after probation or parole commitment has ended.

References

Bratina, M. P. (2013). Sex offender residency requirements: An effective crime prevention strategy or a false sense of security? *Journal of Police Science & Management, 15(3),* 200-218. Doi:10.1350/ijps.2013.15.3.312

Braithwaite, J. (1989). *Crime, shame, and reinte*gration. New York, New York: Cambridge University Press.

Budd, K. M. (2016). Crime control theatre: Public (mis) perceptions of the effectiveness of sex offender residence restrictions. *Psychology, Public Policy, and Law, 22(4),* 362-374. Doi: 10.1037/law0000083

Burchfield, K.B. (2011). Residence restrictions. *Criminology & Public Policy, 10(2),* 411-419. Doi:1111/j.1745-9133.2011.00716.x

Huebner, B.M., Kras, K.R., Rydberg, J. Bynum, T.S., Grommon, E., & Pleggenkuhle, B. (2014). The effect and implications of sex offender residence restrictions: Evidence from a two-state evaluation. *Criminology and Public Policy, 13(1),* 139-160. Doi:10.1111/1745-9133.12066

Jeglic, E.L., Calkins, Levenson, J.S. (2012). The prevelance and correlates of depression and hopelessness among sex offenders subject to community notification and residence restriction legislation. *American Journal of Criminal Justice, 37(1),* 46-59. Doi:10.1007/s12103-010-9096-9

Meloy, M. L., Miller, S .L. & Curtis, K.M. (2008). Making sense out of nonsense: The deconstruction of state-level sex offender residence restrictions. *American Journal of Criminal Justice, 33(2),* 209-222. Doi: 10.1007/512103-008-9042-2

Mustaine, E. E. (2014). Sex offender residency restrictions: Successful integration or Exclusion? *Criminology and Public Policy, 13(1),* 169-177. Doi: 10 1111/1745-9133.12076

Mustaine, E.E., Tewksbury, R., & Stengel, K.M. (2006). Residential location and mobility of egistered sex offenders. *American Journal of Criminal Justice, 30:* 177-192. Doi:10.1007/BF0288590

Rydberg, J., Grommon, E., Huebner, B.M., & Pleggenkuhle, B. (2017). Examining the correlates of sex offender residence restriction violation rates. *Journal of Quantitative Criminology, 33(2),* 347-369. Doi: 10.1007/510940-016-9303-2

Tewksbury, R. (2011). Policy implications of sex offender residence restrictions laws. *Criminology and Public Policy, 10(2).* Doi:10.1111/j.1745-9133.2011.0172.x

Tolson, D., & Klein, J. (2015). Registration, residency restrictions, and community notification: A social capital perspective on the isolation of registered sex offenders in our communities. *Journal of Human Behavior in the Social Environment, 23,* 375-390. Doi:10.1080/10911359.2014.966221

Zgoba, K.M. (2011). Residence restriction buffer zones and the banishment of sex offenders: Have we gone one step too far? *Criminology and Public Policy, 10(2).* 391-400. Doi:10.1111/j.1745-9133.2011.00714.x

Printed in the United States
by Baker & Taylor Publisher Services